FUN WITH OPPOSITES
COLORING BOOK

by Anna Pomaska
and Suzanne Ross

DOVER PUBLICATIONS, INC.
MINEOLA, NEW YORK

Note

How can you show the difference between "big" and "little"? By putting an elephant and a mouse together in a picture, as Anna Pomaska and Suzanne Ross have done in this book! Another page shows a cheerful mouse in a sailboat with an underwater view of his anchor touching the ocean floor; in that scene, you immediately see the difference between "float" and "sink." There are a total of 45 pairs of opposites here, all presented in pictures of children and animals doing many different everyday things. And all of these pictures are ideal for coloring, giving you plenty of fun as you learn these important and frequently used opposite words.

Copyright

Copyright © 1989, 2013 by Dover Publications, Inc.
All rights reserved.

Bibliographical Note

BOOST Fun with Opposites Coloring Book, first published by Dover Publications, Inc., in 2013, is a revised edition of *Fun with Opposites Coloring Book,* originally published by Dover in 1989.

International Standard Book Number

ISBN-13: 978-0-486-49400-5
ISBN-10: 0-486-49400-4

Manufactured in the United States by Courier Corporation
49400401   2013
www.doverpublications.com

TALL

SHORT

 L.K.5.b Demonstrate understanding of frequently occurring verbs and adjectives by relating them to their opposites (antonyms). Also **RI.K.3, RI.K.7, RI.K.10; RF.K.1.**

CCSS **RI.K.3** With prompting and support, describe the connection between two individuals, events, ideas, or pieces of information in a text. Also **RI.K.4, RI.K.7; L.K.5.b, L.K.6.**

 RI.K.7 With prompting and support, describe the relationship between illustrations and the text in which they appear. Also **RI.K.3; RF.K.1.b, RF.K.4; L.K.5.b.**

SHALLOW

DEEP

FAT

THIN

 RI.K.3 With prompting and support, describe the connection between two individuals, events, ideas, or pieces of information in a text. Also **RI.K.7; RF.K.1; L.K.5.b.**

9

 L.K.5.b Demonstrate understanding of frequently occurring verbs and adjectives by relating them to their opposites (antonyms). Also **RI.K.7; RF.K.4; SL.K.4.**

WILD

TAME

RI.K.4 With prompting and support, ask and answer questions about unknown words in a text. Also **RI.K.7; SL.K.2; L.K.5.b, L.K.6.**

IN

OUT

RI.K.10 Actively engage in group reading activities with purpose and understanding. Also
RI.K.7; L.K.1.e, L.K.5.b.

CCSS RI.K.7 With prompting and support, describe the relationship between illustrations and the text in which they appear. Also **RI.K.3; SL.K.4; L.K.5.b.**

CCSS **L.K.5.b** Demonstrate understanding of frequently occurring verbs and adjectives by relating them to their opposites (antonyms). Also **RI.K.7; SL.K.4.**

NEAT

MESSY

CCSS **RI.K.3** With prompting and support, describe the connection between two individuals, events, ideas, or pieces of information in a text. Also **RI.K.7; RF.K.1.b; SL.K.2; L.K.5.b.**

HIGH

LOW

L.K.5.b Demonstrate understanding of frequently occurring verbs and adjectives by relating them to their opposites (antonyms). Also **RI.K.3, RI.K.7; RF.K.1, RF.K.4.**

 RI.K.3 With prompting and support, describe the connection between two individuals, events, ideas, or pieces of information in a text. Also RI.K.7; SL.K.2; L.K.5.b.

SOFT

HARD

CCSS **RI.K.7** With prompting and support, describe the relationship between illustrations and the text in which they appear. Also **RI.K.3; RF.K.1.b; L.K.5.b.**

ROUND

FLAT

CCSS **L.K.5.b** Demonstrate understanding of frequently occurring verbs and adjectives by relating them to their opposites (antonyms). Also **RI.K.7; SL.K.2; L.K.6.**

RI.K.7 With prompting and support, describe the relationship between illustrations and the text in which they appear. Also **RI.K.3; SL.K.2, SL.K.4; L.K.5.b.**

EMPTY

FULL

CCSS **RI.K.3** With prompting and support, describe the connection between two individuals, events, ideas, or pieces of information in a text. Also **RI.K.7; RF.K.1; L.K.5.b, L.K.6.**

LEFT

RIGHT

RI.K.7 With prompting and support, describe the relationship between illustrations and the text in which they appear. Also **RI.K.3; RF.K.1; SL.K.2; L.K.5.b.**

27

SHORT

LONG

 RI.K.3 With prompting and support, describe the connection between two individuals, events, ideas, or pieces of information in a text. Also **RI.K.7; SL.K.4; L.K.5.b.**

CCSS RI.K.10 Actively engage in group reading activities with purpose and understanding. Also RI.K.3, RI.K.7; L.K.5.b, L.K.6.

FRONT

BACK

 L.K.5.b Demonstrate understanding of frequently occurring verbs and adjectives by relating them to their opposites (antonyms). Also **RI.K.7; SL.K.2.**

 RI.K.3 With prompting and support, describe the connection between two individuals, events, ideas, or pieces of information in a text. Also **RI.K.7; L.K.1.e, L.K.5.b.**

 RI.K.3 With prompting and support, describe the connection between two individuals, events, ideas, or pieces of information in a text. Also **RI.K.7; RF.K.3.b; L.K.5.b.**

CCSS **L.K.5.b** Demonstrate understanding of frequently occurring verbs and adjectives by relating them to their opposites (antonyms). Also **RI.K.7; RF.K.3.b, RF.K.4.**

 RI.K.3 With prompting and support, describe the connection between two individuals, events, ideas, or pieces of information in a text. Also **RI.K.7; SL.K.4; L.K.5.b.**

35

CCSS **RI.K.7** With prompting and support, describe the relationship between illustrations and the text in which they appear. Also **RI.K.3; RF.K.3.b; L.K.5.b.**

 RI.K.3 With prompting and support, describe the connection between two individuals, events, ideas, or pieces of information in a text. Also **RI.K.7; SL.K.4; L.K.5.b.**

 RI.K.4 With prompting and support, ask and answer questions about unknown words in a text. Also **RI.K.7; L.K.4, L.K.4.a, L.K.5.b.**

BEFORE

AFTER

 RI.K.7 With prompting and support, describe the relationship between illustrations and the text in which they appear. Also RI.K.3; SL.K.4; L.K.5.b.

CCSS **RI.K.10** Actively engage in group reading activities with purpose and understanding. Also **RI.K.7; L.K.4.b, L.K.5.b.**

 RI.K.7 With prompting and support, describe the relationship between illustrations and the text in which they appear. Also **RI.K.3; SL.K.2; L.K.5.b.**

44

CCSS L.K.5.b Demonstrate understanding of frequently occurring verbs and adjectives by relating them to their opposites (antonyms). Also **RI.K.3, RI.K.7; SL.K.2.**

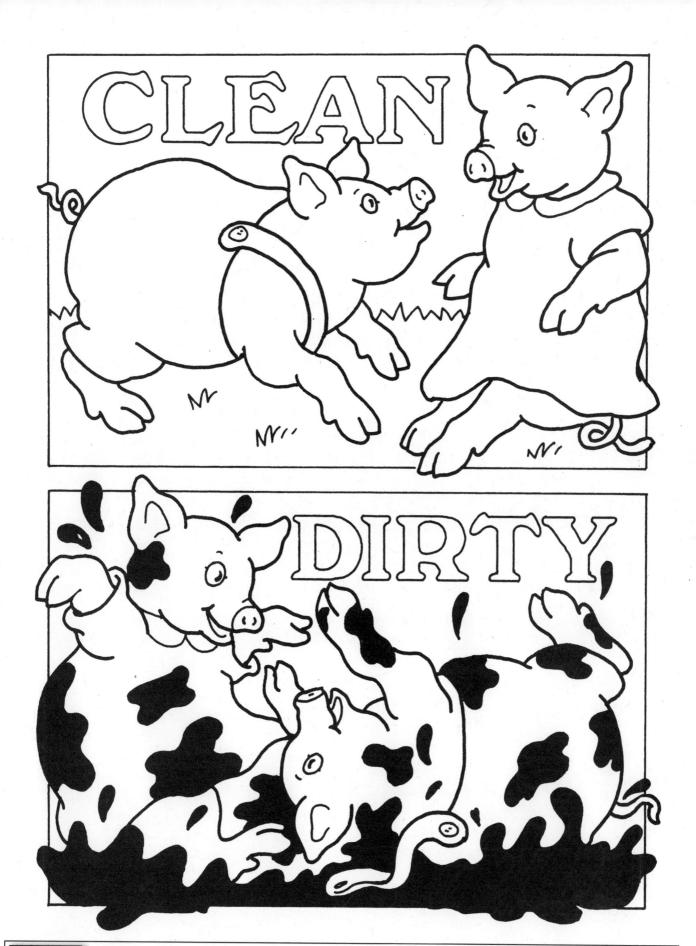